COUSINS

Written by
Mary Ellen Brown Carlson

Illustrations
by Wes Bossman

HARDBACK: 978-1-950256-85-3
PAPERBACK: 978-1-950256-84-6
EBOOK: 978-1-950256-86-0

Ordering Information:

For orders and inquiries, please contact:
1-888-375-9818
www.toplinkpublishing.com
bookorder@toplinkpublishing.com

Printed in the United States of America

DEDICATION

For my husband, Jeff:
Thank you for initiating *Cousins* on paper and
being supportive of my writing endeavors.
You are my rock, I love you.

For my sons, Andrew and Benjamin:
Thank you for always keeping the lighter side of life in my vision.
You are men of strength, integrity, and compassion. I love you both.

For my family, Dad (Charles), Mom (Ruth), Mark, Janel, John, Ricardo and
Wirote: who made the bond of family important with wisdom,
acceptance, laughter and many fun camping excursions, I love you all.

For my grandpas, Clifford and C. Wilner (Bill).
Uncles, Pete, Tom, Albert, Milton and Harold.
Cousins, Paul, Dan, Scott, Bradley, David, Bruce, Terry, Dick, Dale, David, Don,
Randy and Tom.
Father in law, Don. Brother in laws, Don, Joe, Paul and Jim.
Nephews, Sean, Jason, Matthew, Michael, Aaron, Timothy,
John, David and Max:
who have all contributed to making never forgotten family
"memories", I love you all.

For all our military, police, fire and rescue forces: thank you for your service.

"So now faith, hope, and love abide, these three;
but the greatest of these is love."
-1 Corinthians 13:13

To God be the glory for His grace and blessings.

The wall-tent the author's family camped in for many years.
(Set up at a family reunion in 1990)

The original trailer camper used by
author's great grandma and family. (circa. 1898)

Author with siblings and cousins in front of camper using original chassis/frame. (1961)

Author with family and camper with rebuilt frame and canvas sewn by her dad. (1969)

The Brown family continues to have a reunion every three years, where cousins gather to share stories recounting memories of camping trips, reunions and family history.

Author's sons on the infamous tractor owned by the author's father. (1983)

The inseparable cousins, Michael, Aaron, Andrew, Benjamin and Timothy. (1989)

MARY ELLEN BROWN CARLSON

The cousins were two sets of brothers. Let's meet them.

Andrew Carlson

Benjamin Carlson

Aaron Stormer

Timothy Stormer

Every year Andrew, Benny, Aaron and Timmy meet at Grandma and Grandpa Brown's house for a couple of weeks during the summer.

his summer the four boys decided to go camping in the woods behind Grandma and Grandpa Brown's house.

They packed their sleeping bags, crib and tent. Then they loaded them on Grandpa Brown's tractor.

Aaron drove the tractor.

aron drove up the hill and into the woods. The boys decided to make camp down in the bottom of a big gully.

They were really tired by the time they had
finally pitched their tent. They decided to get
into their pajamas and go right to sleep.

MARY ELLEN BROWN CARLSON

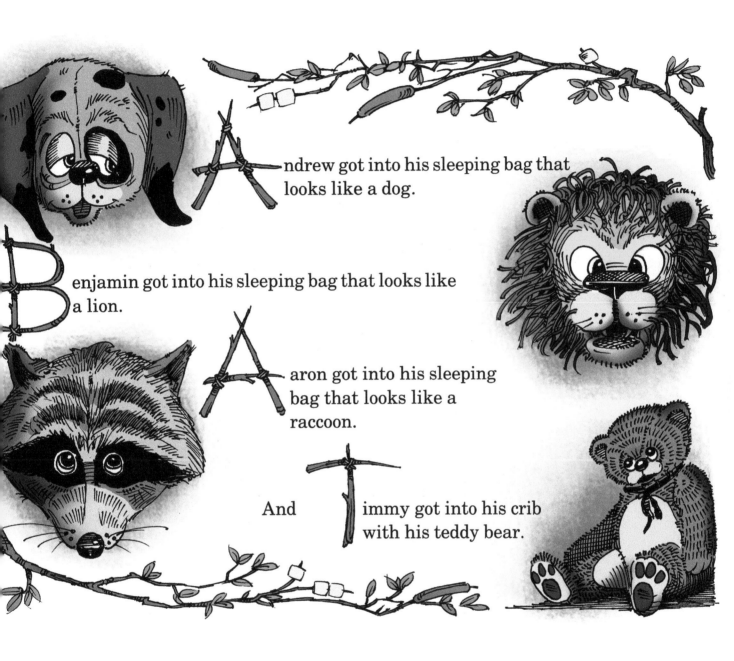

ndrew got into his sleeping bag that looks like a dog.

enjamin got into his sleeping bag that looks like a lion.

aron got into his sleeping bag that looks like a raccoon.

And   immy got into his crib with his teddy bear.

The four boys went fast asleep.
Suddenly there was a
loud noise.
Benny jumped up and
said, "What is that?"

MARY ELLEN BROWN CARLSON

Andrew stuck his head outside of the tent and saw a big "BEAR!" The boys decided they had better lay down in their tent and wait quietly for the bear to go away.

The boys waited for awhile. Benny said, "Is the bear all gone?" Andrew said, "Should we look?" And Timmy said, "A yak a bak a boo!"Aaron looked out of the tent and saw that the bear was gone.

MARY ELLEN BROWN CARLSON

By now the boys were a little scared, so they decided to pack up their camp and head back down to Grandma and Grandpa Brown's house.

They rolled up their sleeping bags, folded up the crib, packed up the tent and loaded their gear on to the tractor.

aron drove them through the woods, down the big hill and up to Grandpa and Grandma Brown's house.

MARY ELLEN BROWN CARLSON

All four went running up to the house and knocked on the door. Grandma and Grandpa came to the door.

The boys said, "There's a bear up there in the woods. Could we sleep in your house tonight?"

"Why certainly," said Grandma Brown as she let the boys into the house. The boys went straight into the bedroom and quietly slept for the rest of the night. The End.

CPSIA information can be obtained
at www.ICGtesting.com
Printed in the USA
BVHW020231270219
541212BV00008B/17/P